Coexisting

with...

Agoraphobia, Anxiety

&

Panic Attacks

A Handbook By Ellen Isaksen

Coexisting with...
Agoraphobia, Anxiety & Panic Attacks

Printed in the United States of America

ISBN-13: 978-1503244207
ISBN-10: 1503244202

FOREWORD

U sually the Foreword of a book is reserved for experts with massive amounts of very official-looking letters following his or her name and some pretty impressive professional titles. I have neither. Well, I guess if I had to give myself a title, it would be "Professional Scared Person." And I certainly consider myself an expert on the subject of anxiety disorders, having both a degree in psychology and lived with agoraphobia my entire adult life. I have also been housebound with this disorder since 1986. My other qualification for writing this is that Ellen and I have been close friends for well over 25 years, even though we have never met in person. Could agoraphobia be the mother of invention? I think so...

Okay, enough about me. After all, I am supposed to be saying wonderful things about Ellen and her wonderful book. And they both are. Anyone suffering from any type of anxiety disorder, from a simple phobia to full-blown agoraphobia can find a mountain of useful information between these covers (virtual or otherwise). She has broken down the psycho-babble and created a handbook that is easy to comprehend, humorous and ultimately readable. Ellen not only talks the talk, she has walked the walk. Having had most of the same struggles as Ellen, I can easily identify with just about everything she addresses. What is especially vital to me is this book's relevance to fellow sufferers, no matter what stage of recovery they are in. Her most important message is pure and simple: Accept yourself whatever your limitations and build a life despite them.

And that is a very powerful message...

Luci Waddell
Professional Scared Person

TABLE OF CONTENTS

Foreword iii

Acknowledgements .... g

Introduction 1

Symptoms 11

Feelings... Oh, Oh, Oh Feelings! 19

Quirks 33

Avoidance 53

Making it Work 57

Systematic Desensitization 73

The Toolbox 83

Always Improving 101

Suggested Reading 111

ACKNOWLEDGEMENTS

This book came about as a result of a series of interviews that I did with a reporter from the *Tampa Bay Times* by the name of Zack Peterson. Zack discovered my first book, *Behind These Eyes: One Agoraphobic's Journey To A Meaningful Life* online and asked me if I'd be willing to talk to him about my book and my life. I agreed and had to spend long periods of time examining my life and how I made it work. The information in this book as well as my YouTube videos are a result of that introspection and those interviews. Thank you Zack for getting the ball rolling!

I would also like to thank Nat for her wonderful work in formatting this book (as well as my memoir) so that they might appear in a readable manner for public presentation. Her job is indeed not for the faint of heart! Nat always goes the extra mile and throws in a hefty dose of patience and good-naturedness for good measure. She lives in Croatia and came to me as a result of an online search for someone to assist me with the daunting task of getting all my material ready for publication both in print and as an eBook. She is a wizard and a blessing! Thank you *so* much Nat...may you always be performing your valuable service. I know you think you are only tech support, but you are *so* much more than that to me!

Next, I'd like to thank my good friend and editor, Luci Waddell for her *endless* valuable input. She worked with me on both books as well and always helps to make my words sound so much smarter than they started out! We are both agoraphobic and have an understanding that goes beyond words.

A very special thank you goes out to my dear Julie for not giving up on her search until she found me.

Ultimately, I'd like to give thanks to The Universe. I am blessed in so many ways.

INTRODUCTION

Hi, my name is Ellen Isaksen and I would like to talk to you about what it is like to live life as an agoraphobic. Initially, I will be giving you a brief background about myself and what exactly agoraphobia is. Please be advised that anything mentioned here is only information about myself that I am sharing in hopes that some of it might be helpful to you. It is not meant as a recommendation that you adjust your life in any way. My main qualification is the fact that I have lived personally with anxiety and agoraphobia for over five decades. Please just take the best and leave the rest.

Agoraphobia is a type of anxiety disorder in which you fear, and usually avoid, places or situations that might cause your anxiety levels to rise, often to the point of panic, or that make you feel trapped or helpless. The reaction to these places and/or circumstances may increase in number and intensity over time and become so strong and terrifying that you eventually avoid them completely. Ultimately you begin to avoid all outside situations for fear that you might have a reaction and you remain within the confines of your home or safe place. Finally, the mere anticipation of having an anxiety reaction or panic attack is enough to keep you from venturing out. This is what Dr. Claire Weekes, a pioneer in the field of agoraphobia, calls Second Fear, which adds an additional difficulty to the original problem of the actual panic or anxiety reaction. There is much written about agoraphobia these days so I won't spend much time on technical data, but rather would like to share with you what it is actually like to live one's life as an agoraphobic from the agoraphobic's point of view. I have plenty of experience with it since, as I mentioned, I myself have been challenged with severe anxiety, panic and agoraphobic since about age 13. I have also dealt with it from the other side of the desk as a counselor. I am now 66 years old and have managed to live a relatively productive life of coexistence with my challenge, especially since I gave up the idea that I had to be like everyone else in order to have any semblance of a "normal" life. I finally got to a point where I simply made peace with my life as it was and decided to just play the hand I was dealt.

While I totally support whatever effort is being taken to overcome anxiety and fears, my main focus is on those challenged with the most severe forms of anxiety and agoraphobia and for whom standard therapies and medications have not produced the desired results. I believe this will also be extremely helpful information for those who need coping skills while undergoing their current method of treatment. I fell between the cracks in the medical community and went over twenty years undiagnosed. I had so many years, decades even where I developed conditioned responses to my anxiety and that conditioning was very difficult to overcome. You need not fear that happening to you however, as there is so much more known about agoraphobia today and there are always new medications and therapies on the horizon. Back in the early 60's when I had my first *major* episode with panic and agoraphobia, the disorder was not recognized. I went from a stable, honors student in grammar school and early high school to a homebound teenager in what seemed to be the blink of an eye! But I am here to tell you that a full and meaningful life can still be had even after such an experience. While I have never fully recovered, I have had a life with many interesting and rewarding twists and turns, and ultimately even ended up having a career as a Psychiatric Social Worker. I have had many good friends and personal relationships as well. It seemed however, that I'd just work my way into the outside world and then something would happen and I'd end up housebound again. For the almost eighteen years while I was getting my college degrees and working full time in the outside world, I relied upon alcohol to function. Thankfully, around 1982 I managed to give up alcohol completely. My book, *Behind These Eyes: One Agoraphobic's Journey to a Meaningful Life* chronicles that entire process. I was eventually forced to face my world with anxiety without any crutches. I knew I'd end up dead if I continued drinking at the rate I had been going.

There has been much trauma and loss in my life and those events have been major contributing factors to my inability to stay comfortably in the world beyond my home. It should be noted that even though I am in my home, I am not necessarily relaxed and at peace. High anxiety and panic can hit anywhere, at any time, often seeming to come out of the blue. I have tried many types of therapy including supportive, cognitive and systematic desensitization. All of these treatments helped me get out of my house for certain intervals, but eventually I'd find myself limited to my home once

4

again. For decades I tried putting that key in the car ignition every day just to see if I could get around the corner. In later years most times I didn't and then I'd beat myself up and get depressed and feel so much less than everyone else. After all, the whole world seems to define how normal you are by what you do, how much you have and where you can go. If you cannot even get to the grocery store surely you are severely mentally ill!

In the year 2000 I made a conscious decision to try to develop my spirituality. I never had a strong religious upbringing and was somehow jealous of those who could rely on their faith to get them through tough times. I decided to explore certain beliefs and see if anything was a fit for me. One day, while reading something about Buddhism, I realized that what was truly most important in this world was who I was inside and what I could give of myself to others. My worth as a human being had nothing to do with where I could or could not go or what I could or could not do. I thought, "If that be true, than I can be a total and complete person even if I never left my chair!" I felt so very free from that moment on. I simply gave up the *need* to have to put that key in the ignition every day. If the spirit moved me, I headed for the car. If not, I didn't give it a second thought. I decided to focus my days positively, concentrating on what I could do and not on what I apparently could not. It almost seemed like insanity for not thinking of this sooner! From that moment on I got up in the morning happily planning what I truly *wanted* to do with my day. I began developing an online business doing custom printing. This was a carryover from days gone by when I actually owned a T shirt shop. I learned how to do web page design and made many online contacts. A whole new world opened up for me when I got my first computer. I discovered that I possessed many different kinds of creative talent. I felt alive for the first time in years! I continued with my therapy sessions with my counselor, but I had shifted my focus away from the negativity of how much anxiety I was experiencing and all the things I could not do and how terrible I felt about myself for not being able to function as what the rest of the world considered normal. Life began to change as I decided to discover my own definition of "normal." I had not given up; I just knew in my heart that to date I had tried everything I could think of to keep myself in the outside world and I had lost myself to that singular goal. Life was passing me by and I was not getting any younger. It was at that point that I created the first *real* life I had ever known for myself; a different kind of life than most people embraced. I never looked back.

Today I still live with frequent high levels of

anxiety and am at this moment housebound. Recently, I have experienced many changes and losses in my life and am in the process of reinventing myself once again. My first book was the beginning of that reinvention, even though I didn't realize it at the time. Initially I wrote my autobiography because I thought I had a story to tell as well as the hope that it might help someone who could identify with my challenge. *Behind These Eyes* is a very complete account of my life virtually from birth until about two years ago. I describe some early childhood neglect and abuse which probably laid the foundation for my insecurities and anxiety about living in this world. From there I describe my first major incident with anxiety and panic at about age 13. From that moment I became immediately homebound and could barely even leave my room. My meals were literally slipped under the door of my bedroom for a long time. I was petrified to even look out my bedroom window. The rest of the book is basically about how I learned to live with my anxiety and panic. With the exception of the first two years I spent in college, I have had to deal with some degree of anxiety and panic almost on a daily basis, along with social phobia and many of the other idiosyncrasies that can go along with anxiety disorders. My plan was to go back to my life after writing the book and try again to just let my anxiety run in the background and not focus much on it and live my day. Life, however, took an interesting turn.

Following the publication of *Behind These Eyes*, a reporter from the *Tampa Bay Times* contacted me in regard to writing an article. He had found my book online and asked if I'd consider being interviewed for a piece in the *Times* about the book and my life. Once we completed multiple interviews, it occurred to me that all the information I shared with him might be helpful to others. At that point, I decided to take a stab at making a few videos on YouTube. Doing the abovementioned article has forced me to think long and hard about how I manage to live my life on a daily basis; how I manage despite my anxiety to have a fairly big life. Again, I believe all this scrutiny may be of help to others. In subsequent chapters, I hope to cover in a very detailed manner all the coping skills I have managed to discover and develop. I do not intend to linger on the symptoms of anxiety per se; people with anxiety disorders are very suggestible and focusing on the physiological aspect of agoraphobia can sometimes cause one to develop symptoms not previously experienced. I will discuss them briefly and move on. The bottom line here is that they are all just that: a physical reaction to a stimulus and can be dealt with by simply accepting that they are there and working our lives around them. Thinking too much about symptoms just gives them needless power. Much information is also on my website at http://living-wth-agoraphobia.com where I offer a blog, tools for coping and much more.

My intentions in writing this book are:

1. To encourage those who feel that they cannot have any kind of productive life if they are a homebound agoraphobic or are living with high levels of anxiety on a regular basis.

2. To offer real insight from an agoraphobic's point of view about how it really is living with agoraphobia and ongoing anxiety.

3. To help loved ones of those with agoraphobia by allowing them to see how real all these symptoms are and how debilitating they can be; to help them to understand that we are not faking, especially when we can do something one day or even one minute and not the next.

4. To offer specific coping skills for dealing with symptoms to get through certain life situations.

5. To offer suggested readings.

6. To offer creative coping tips that can simply make life easier.

As you read this little handbook, you will find multiple redundancies. This is intentional! Some of this information is important enough to bear repeating. And being the type of people who suffer from a natural incredulity, sometimes we need to hear things repeatedly before we actually start to believe them.

Symptoms

While there is nothing to be gained by dwelling on the symptoms of anxiety, I feel it's important to list them in their hierarchy on the anxiety scale. I will also discuss the causes of these symptoms in order to demystify them for you so maybe they won't seem so terribly frightening. I do this in the hopes that if you experience a new symptom, you can identify it as anxiety and not the heart attack/stroke/rickets/whatever you fear it to be. However, it is always important to see a doctor for a physical exam to ensure that what you are feeling is, in fact, anxiety. I am not a physician and am in no way attempting to diagnose.

Having said that, it is important not to dwell on or obsess about symptoms. The reason for this is that phobics are extremely suggestible and while you may not have all the symptoms listed, focusing on this list may add them to your repertoire! Read the list, say, "Yeah, that's me!" and move on. "Symptom-dwelling" is mightily discouraged for this reason. Start thinking of your symptoms in terms of its number on the anxiety scale as opposed to the symptom itself and you'll find it easier to deal with.

According to Edmund Bourne, Ph.D., the anxiety scale is as follows:

The Anxiety Scale

1. Butterflies in stomach.

2. Sweaty or clammy palms, warmth all over.

3. Rapid or strong heartbeat, tremor, mild muscle tension.

4. Shaky legs, "weak in the knees" sensation, tremors.

5. Dry mouth, feeling the need for escape.

6. Lump in throat, more severe muscle tension.

7. Tight chest, hyperventilation.

8. Stiff neck, headache, feelings of doom.

9. Dizziness, nausea, diarrhea, visual distortions, numbness or tingling, concern for losing control.

10. Disorientation, "spaciness," detached, frantic,

hysterical numbness, weird sensations and/or feelings.

Okay, there you have it. Now let's break it down:

1. 1 - 3 is normal anxiety. Everyone gets this and no matter how hard you try, you're stuck with these forever. Welcome to the human race!

2. 4 - 6 is the area of decreased ability to function. You are more keenly aware that something is wrong.

3. 7 - 9 is the area of non-function. By this time, it's nearly impossible to concentrate on anything other than your symptoms.

4. 10 is full-blown panic.

As I mentioned earlier, start thinking in terms of your symptoms as numbers. Telling yourself, "I'm at a 6 now." is a lot less scary than telling yourself your throat is closing up (which it isn't).

What causes these symptoms to escalate is adding the "second fear" or "what if?" Chances are, if you are feeling a tightness in your chest and you start thinking in terms of a heart attack, you'll scare yourself silly and the symptoms will increase. If you understand the physiological reasons for the sensations you are experiencing and the fact that they are **not dangerous**, that will go a long way toward decreasing your anxiety.

Let's talk about a few of those second fears and hopefully lay them to rest:

1. **A panic attack cannot cause heart failure or cardiac arrest**

   Increased heart rate and palpitations are very frightening, but they are not dangerous. According to Claire Weekes, a healthy heart can sustain a heart rate of 200 beats per minute for days or even weeks without damage.

2. **A panic attack will not cause you to stop breathing or suffocate**

   It is a very common symptom during a panic attack to have the sensation of your chest and throat tightening and your breathing to become restricted. Rest assured that there is nothing wrong with your breathing passages; what you are experiencing is a result of the severe muscle tension in your neck and chest.

3. **A panic attack cannot cause you to faint**

   What is happening when you experience that sensation of light-headedness is the blood flow to your brain is *slightly* (make a note of that "slightly," please!) reduced, most likely due to the rapidity of your breathing. Try taking slow, deep breaths and this will clear up. The fact that your heart is actually pumping harder and increasing your circulation precludes fainting. If you do faint, it is because of hyperventilation, *not* the panic attack.

4. A panic attack cannot cause you to fall over

The adrenaline released during a panic attack dilates the blood vessels in your legs, causing a "weak in the knees" feeling. Not to worry: your legs are as strong as they were before and this is only a sensation.

5. You won't go crazy during a panic attack

I think this is the best news of all! Reduced flow of blood to your brain during a panic attack is due to arterial constriction, a *normal* side-effect of rapid breathing. This can result in feelings of disorientation and unreality that can be very frightening. But trust me on this one, you're still sane!

6. A panic attack cannot cause you to lose control

Because of the intensity of the feelings you are experiencing, it's quite easy to picture yourself totally losing it. If anything, during a panic attack your senses are all heightened with the sole thought in mind of fight or flight. Losing control during a panic attack is sheer myth.

The first step in learning how to cope with panic attacks is to understand the body reactions you are having are *not* dangerous. Actually, the physiological reactions brought about by a panic attack are natural and protective. Keep this thought firmly in mind.

Agoraphobia is caused by a combination of heredity and environment, or *nature versus nurture*. It is a behavioral disorder, although it is classified as a mental illness. There are those people with personalities pre-disposed to being phobic. We are highly intelligent, creative, imaginative, and sensitive (and no, "sensitive" is NOT a bad word!) We have many, many sterling qualities and are viable, productive and useful members of society. We are very loving, kind, compassionate, and caring. We are "people" persons, always willing to give and give of ourselves. And these are NOT bad things!

The good news is that you can learn to live with your anxiety disorder. You do *not* have to relegate yourself to the attic and become crazy Aunt Hattie who no one ever sees. This process is a slow one, but look how long it took you to get to this point! You can learn coping strategies that will allow you to feel more comfortable in your surroundings. You can get a better understanding of your condition, which will facilitate the healing process. And most importantly, you will once again feel like you are a viable member of the human race, not to be discounted simply because you have a few limitations. You are NOT your symptoms!

Feelings... Oh, Oh, Oh Feelings!

Because we are highly sensitive people, many agoraphobics and those suffering from anxiety disorders in general tend to experience feelings very intensely. Additionally, if you come from an abusive or neglectful background or a household with rigid rules, you may have felt the necessity to hide your feelings. You may have had the experience of feeling an emotion so intensely that it actually frightened you. The good news is that actually *feeling* the feelings, no matter how extreme, is always much healthier than trying to sit on them. It is also true that releasing those volatile feelings helps to reduce anxiety. Of course, if they are so-called negative feelings, such as anger or rage, we need to be careful to express them in an appropriate way and not release them on innocent bystanders.

I think this section of the book is so important because anxiety and panic attacks are mostly all about negative thoughts creating strong FEELINGS. There is a biological component for sure, but here I am referring to those times when we manufacture such negative thoughts that they can throw us into a real tizzy. It was enlightening and somewhat encouraging to me to discover that feelings are just energy! We need to try to not be guided solely by our feelings, but learn to identify when they are just automatic responses that need to be accepted as such and simply moved through so we can go on living our lives. It is important to know that feelings are meant to be *felt* and *passed through*. Sometimes, however, they are telling us that we are on the wrong path and need to do something differently. It can be challenging to know the difference.

For instance, since I am socially phobic, planning to meet someone new can trigger habitual stressful and anxious feelings. I have been reacting this way for so long I have to believe that a large part of it is habit and I need to just feel those feelings and let them go. On the other hand, I can start to tense up and get anxious for no apparent reason. At that point I have to stop and think back on recent events to see if there is an unresolved issue still troubling me that needs addressing. This is a process of indeterminate length; it could take an hour, it could take a week. This is actually good news for me, as it used to sometimes take years for me to identify the underlying cause. When I start to experience this type of unspecified anxiety, I know I have to set some time aside and allow myself to simply be quietly alone to see what surfaces. The trigger is not necessarily the first thought that comes to mind; it may be something more deep-seeded that requires further contemplation. I know I am on the right track when I feel my body begin to relax. It can be frustrating to have to live this way, but it simply is what *is* and I have learned to accept my sensitive nature and even honor it. Please keep in mind that this personality trait has its rewards as well. While I feel anxiety, anger and pain to a greater degree than the non-phobic person, I also experience joy, love and compassion to an equally greater degree. In addition, I am also much more empathetic to others who have their own challenges in life.

However, there is also a little thing called stress that comes into play. Welcome to the human race, we all experience stress of one kind or another, and to varying degrees. Good stress or bad stress, it can all *feel* the same. For example, at the time of this writing I have been undergoing some very positive changes in my life. There are new people surrounding me, there is the possibility of new business opportunities opening up for me, I am feeling especially creative and life is generally good. However, this too can cause me to feel overwhelmed and consequently anxious. My finely tuned nervous system reacts at the smallest *exciting* thought the same way as it does to a scary thought or situation. My body gets alerted to some new stimuli and it is off and running! For me, once that adrenalin switch is turned on it can take a long time to turn it off. I can stay hyped up for days and it can take just as many days to feel relief. This entire process is exhausting and it can take the fun out of having fun! I often feel as if my body betrays me. I can be thoroughly looking forward to an event, expecting to have a nice time and then when the event actually comes to pass, POW! I get hit with a truckload of anxiety! This happens most times when I am dealing with situations involving other people. As mentioned previously, I am socially phobic, which seems so odd even to me because I have such an outgoing personality. Even though I really *want* to see someone, my body reacts with *great* excitement or *great* anxiety and can make my visit miserable. This is where pure biology must come in, because I am thinking good thoughts and having a positive attitude, but my body gets triggered in an exaggerated way and I am spinning like a Whirling Dervish. This just might be the most frustrating aspect of the disorder for me.

Feelings *feel* real, and indeed they are very real. They can propel us into taking action; they can make us smile or laugh. They can even make us cry or run to take cover. When we lack any feeling we are numb, depressed or not truly alive. Not feeling alive is no fun either! However, one of the things that I have learned about feelings is that they can be very deceiving. While they feel real enough, they may be sending messages that are not true which can cause us even more misery. We may be frustrated with ourselves for something we cannot do and *feel* inadequate and that can easily translate to the thought that we *are* inadequate, which is simply not true! Feeling inadequate and *being* inadequate are two different animals. I was listening to Tara Brach, a leading western teacher of Buddhist meditation, emotional healing and spiritual awakening recently, and she spoke to this concept. She suggested that much of what we feel is based on old buttons from childhood being pushed which makes many of our reactions truly not our fault. This is not to say that we don't need to work on realizing this and modifying our reactions where we can, but we need not beat ourselves up for what we feel and how we respond. We can slowly learn to take charge of our adult behavior and reactions, but this takes time and dedicated practice. It is not easy. Scars from abuse and behaviors passed down to us from our family history can linger for years until we actively decide to find a way to address them. Learning to love ourselves completely, despite our flaws, is key to healing and developing effective coping skills.

One of the not-so-wonderful physical manifestations of anxiety is muscle tension. For some of us, including myself, this can be very problematic. It sounds like a simple thing but again, because we are hypersensitive individuals, muscle tension and the resulting stress knots or trigger points (often brought on by negative thinking) can be overwhelmingly painful. I have been dealing with severe episodes of muscle tension since the late 80s. It took me a long time to realize that this was actually a manifestation of my anxiety disorder. It is certainly not pleasant to feel tense so much of the time. There was an extremely long period of time when I stayed in a constant state of grueling muscle tension. It was so bad that whenever I spoke to my counselor about it I had to abbreviate it to the letters "MTC" (for muscle tension crap) because even just saying the words seemed to make me even tenser! I have come to know that for me, muscle tension to that degree means that either I am sitting on some kind of potent anger issue or that I am significantly off course and I need to sit down and look at where I am and what I should be doing with my life. Looking very honestly at my inner self seems to be the only thing that offers me any relief. These days the bouts are not as severe or as long-lasting, but they always mean I have something to look at deep within. Often, they mean I am too externally focused and I need to slow down and spend time with me. For me the antidote for "MTC" is being real and continuing on my search for my authentic self. Being tense keeps the negative feelings in and the good feelings out. It creates an invisible barrier between us and the outside world. Essentially, we freeze and being numb in the world can be just as painful and scary as taking the leap and putting ourselves out there any way we can.

Learning to cope with our often overwhelming feelings can be challenging indeed. Here are a few things that I have learned that help:

1. Just letting feelings be gives them less power than trying to fight them or force them to go away.

2. Becoming introspective can give the meaning behind the intense feelings an

opportunity to surface. Once I know the underlying purpose of the feelings, I can usually address the issue and subsequently calm down.

3. Feelings are just energy and cannot hurt me.

4. Talking about what I am feeling to someone I trust and who is willing to be an objective listener always helps.

5. Feelings are a necessary part of everyone's life; ours are just a little more intense.

6. Loving and accepting myself no matter how I feel always helps me cope with most anything.

7. Trying to stay focused on positive things in the present moment can help ward off the negative feelings or anxiety that come about from reflecting on a painful past or worry about an unpredictable future.

8. It's easy to link strong emotions with daily events. This can lead to avoidance behavior in the same way as having a panic attack in a specific situation can lead to avoiding that situation. For example, there were times when I had severe muscle tension while watching dancing events on TV so I eventually stopped watching all dancing

shows. That was sad because I really enjoyed them. It took a long time to convince myself that there was absolutely no connection!

9. Spending quiet time outside can help clear your head and emotions and bring inner peace. The sound of birds chirping or the feel of the warm sunshine can bring joy to the weary soul. You don't need to go far, perhaps like me, just enjoy your porch or backyard!

10. It is better to have a smorgasbord of feelings than no feelings at all. There was a time when I was either completely numb or felt only anxiety. That was not a worthwhile existence. These days I know what it feels like to experience anger, rage, joy, passion, excitement, frustration and the full gamut of emotions. There are many of us who feel all choked up with emotion, but really don't know exactly what it is we are feeling. If that applies to you, I suggest you write out a list of all possible feelings and try daily to identify what it is you are experiencing. Identifying the feeling is the jumping-off place to being able to handle the emotion.

11. I am like the princess in *The Princess and the Pea* story. Because I am so sensitive I know I overreact easily. Armed simply with that knowledge, I have a better perspective about my feelings and can often keep myself from responding inappropriately. I try to stop before acting and double-check myself to see if my reaction is really warranted. Thinking before acting is a good rule of thumb for anyone, not just those of us with anxiety challenges. Once again, the good news is that my sensitivity makes me in many respects a valuable and empathetic friend, partner and member of society.

12. One of the most feared and avoided of all emotions is anger. This is due, in part, to the necessity of confrontation in order to appropriately express one's anger. Another aspect of the fear of anger is the possibility of alienating the person to whom your anger is directed. Since we are already so isolated, the thought of losing a friend or loved one is unbearable to most of us. So we stuff the anger and then despise ourselves for being a doormat. Stuffing anger (or any emotion, for that matter) is one of the greatest causes for anxiety.

13. There also exists the scenario in which it is not possible to express one's anger to the applicable person. My friend Luci lost her husband very suddenly some years ago. After the initial onslaught of devastation and grief, she experienced an overwhelming sense of anger. She felt abandoned by him, and was enraged by the reality that she would now be raising their young daughter as a single parent. This additional challenge, coupled with her agoraphobia and grief, was overwhelming. Obviously, she could no longer yell and scream and jump up and down at her husband, so she had to find a different way to successfully vent her anger before it consumed her.

A very effective way to resolve this conundrum is by writing angry letters. This practice is quite simple: Sit down with a large pad of paper and the writing implement of your choice and just WRITE. Let it all spew out, pure stream of consciousness, with no editing. Write out all the nasty, hateful things you are feeling, and then write some more. Compose this as a letter to the person at whom your anger is directed and KEEP WRITING. Write until your hand cramps and KEEP WRITING. Initially, this may be difficult for you and you may only be able to write a sentence or two. No worries; this exercise is rarely accomplished in one sitting. You will probably find that it can take many, many letters to exhaust your anger. Once you have written the letter DO NOT MAIL IT! This is important enough to repeat: DO NOT MAIL IT! Obviously, if you are writing to someone who is deceased, this is not even possible. But this exercise works very well when having to express anger to anyone. Once the letter is completed, destroy it. You can do this by tearing it into dozens of tiny pieces. Luci likes to burn hers; she gets the feeling of releasing all that negativity to be absorbed back into The Universe as she watches the ashes fly upward. This is cathartic, this is healthy, this is effective. And it is also very non-threatening. You never have to openly confront the person with whom you are angry but you are still able to express those feelings.

14. If you put a person under a lot of pressure (and we often feel like we are under a great deal of pressure to perform more "normally") what emerges is what is truly

within. Wayne Dyer once made the analogy that if you squeeze an orange what comes out is orange juice because that is what is naturally inside. For us, there can be a lot of high-powered emotions deep within. We need to be patient, kind and loving with ourselves when what materializes is fear, negative thinking, anger, rage or frustration. Most of us have had to endure a lot of pain in our lives, so it is difficult for us to be happy-go-lucky. As we learn to love and accept ourselves *as is* and move forward with our lives, more peace and joy will surface. This is most definitely a process. It takes dedication and daily practice, but we are worth all the effort we put into ourselves!

15. Most any kind of change can wreak emotional havoc in the life of someone challenged with an anxiety disorder. The key is to try to ride out the emotions long enough so that the change can become the norm. You will not only accomplish your goal, but your self-esteem will grow as well.

16. We are people who can get easily frustrated at how long it might take to accomplish something. It may take us 2 or 5 or 10 more

steps to accomplish what many can do in one, but we surely can accomplish what we want to if we only persevere.

17. Thoughts are creative. Think good thoughts and you will create good feelings!

If you say *YES!* to your life and continue going forward no matter what your fear and emotions throw at you, you will be one of life's unsung heroes. Love yourself exquisitely, without reservation, and you will feel a shift in how you feel about yourself and the world around you.

QUIRKS

I'd like to start this section by saying that I am not offering a cure here but rather, just as the title *Coexisting with Agoraphobia, Anxiety and Panic Attacks* implies, I am trying to offer ways to live alongside the anxiety, making room for it to just *be* while it is happening. To suggest that you embrace it might seem somewhat counterproductive, but that's the general idea. This is not to imply that the anxiety will be a permanent part of your life; realistically, you may find a method that works for your recovery. All that I am trying to say is to accept your life as is, right now, today, while you find your way toward healing. Swimming upstream and fighting against the flow only seems to work for salmon!

In a previous section, you learned that I have been living with this challenge for over five decades. I have been all over the place with it, in and out and everything in between. I mentioned that there was even a time in my younger days when I had to have my meals slipped to me under my bedroom door because I was so terrified of the outside world, which, to me, included everything outside my bedroom. I've come a long way since those days, but am still challenged with this disorder. The difference now is that I know what I have and after trying so many different remedies that didn't work, I have simply made peace with it.

In the Introduction, I mentioned the fact that I functioned for a long time in the outside world by abusing alcohol. *Behind These Eyes* goes into greater depth in regard to this self-destructive path. I spent a short time in my career as a counselor working in a cocaine rehab unit and I am here to tell you that abusing substances is not the answer; it only creates another problem. Unfortunately, it took over 25 years for me to be properly diagnosed as an agoraphobic and I used alcohol during that time to self-medicate. Fortunately, this discovery allowed me to give up the alcohol and pursue other methods to help myself.

I expect this handbook will be akin to a journal; part informational and part accounts of actual events in my life. In this section, I will be discussing quirks, traits or idiosyncrasies that are typical to many people who suffer with anxiety disorders. We have been known to be a little quirky!...

1. Many agoraphobics will not take medication. In my case, I became medication-phobic in the 70's after experiencing many adverse reactions to the drugs I was prescribed. We generally have very susceptible nervous systems and various other sensitivities. For me, reactiveness to drugs is one of them. When I have to try to take a new medication, the best way for me to ease into it is to actually shave the pill with a razor and take it in tiny increments until I am assured that I will not have a reaction to the medication. Another option is to dip your finger into a small amount of the powder of the pill and put a little on your tongue. You can than proceed onto larger amounts until you are comfortable taking the full dosage. Doing things in small increments or baby steps seems to work best with us for most things.

2. We feel the need for control in certain circumstances, especially in situations with which we are unfamiliar. For many—but not all—of us, we have had times when we felt control of our lives was not in our hands.

We may have been abused, had a serious illness or experienced other trauma. I believe that is at the bottom of many of our fears. Today if we are in a situation where we feel we have no choices or feel trapped in any way, we panic. When we undergo that out-of-control feeling, it is helpful to constantly remind ourselves that we are adults today and have complete control over our lives. I always like to point out that we are *not* trying to control other people, even though it may appear that way at times. We are simply trying to arrange the situation (which may include other people) in such a way as to be the least threatening for us. If we can't see it as manageable in our minds then we simply cannot do it, so we need to take steps to lay things out in a manner that makes us able to envision it as possible. There is a very definite, albeit subtle, difference, but a very important difference and one I hope others will be willing to accept.

3. We can feel trapped in the most common of confining places—even in our own home— such as the shower, dinner table, elevator, talking to visitors or neighbors, waiting in supermarket lines and the doctor's office .

We can feel trapped in most any "have to" situation where we feel we *must* do something and have no way out. Ordinary everyday tasks can also cause us much anxiety if we feel confined by them.

4. Light/sun, heat/cold and loud sounds can also trigger an anxiety reaction. Since I am a person who can react strongly to those environmental factors, especially if they change quickly, I was so relieved to find out that light, temperature and sound sensitivity was common for people with anxiety disorders. I live in Florida and at times just walking out to the mailbox can trigger anxiety. Fluorescent lights in stores can also offer enormous stimuli. Many phobics have difficulty at sunrise and sunset. In my case, even the momentary passage of a cloud over the sun can quickly change my mood from calm and peaceful to scary. We are extremely sensitive people who can easily be overstimulated by the most mundane occurrences. We need not be ashamed of this; it is simply the way we are wired. The more we recognize and accept this, the better we will be able to make friends with ourselves.

5. We often need to do things or even see people in small increments. This is commonly known as "baby steps" and again relates to how easily we can get emotionally overstimulated. If we are socially phobic we may need for people to come and visit for only short periods of time, especially if they are unfamiliar to us. If we are trying to do a task we could not do before, such as driving, we may need to attempt this in tiny increments in order to be ultimately successful. This also applies to household chores and other tasks we must perform on a daily basis—anything that is considered a have-to as opposed to a want-to. Baby steps are a great tool here as well. For example, at times even cooking a simple meal can seem daunting. You might feel trapped and unable to escape the kitchen. Try cooking less complicated meals, or ones that can be prepared in steps so you can allow yourself to leave for a few minutes. I will address this approach in greater depth in an up-coming chapter.

6. *Everything* we do is overshadowed by anxiety; the first thought in any given situation is, "How much anxiety will this trigger?" We have to consider the

consequences anxiety-wise inherent in almost everything we do prior to taking action. There is usually no such thing as spontaneity in our situation; everything must be carefully planned out and manipulated in order to cause the least discomfort. We live with the overt fear of being forced into a situation that will remove us from our safe place as well as the underlying fear that on any given day we will experience something that will mentally bring us back to times in our lives when we were at our very worst anxiety-wise. If it is not in the forefront of our minds, it is a constant undercurrent. It can be exhausting.

7. Sometimes anxiety is the only emotion we *can* feel and is used to mask other, more intense emotions. This is a deep-seeded defense mechanism used by our minds to protect us from more profound and unsettling feelings, such as anger or resentment. Learning to identify and experience all of your feelings can be very helpful in helping anxiety to ease.

8. We are constantly attuned to the subtle— and sometimes not so subtle!—shifts in the way we feel and the symptoms we exhibit.

This can be a very self-centered disorder. It is a state of hyper-vigilance, always prepared for your body to betray you and throw you into panic. Often it seems to come totally out of the blue. Triggers can be unconscious; I am as surprised as anyone sometimes when I get so nervous in a situation that I was perhaps even looking forward to! I am not focusing on the possibility that this might be a scary or horrible situation. I just go about my day, looking forward to an event of some kind and then BAM! I can be overwhelmed with anxiety. It can sometimes take days to recover from one of these incidences.

9. One of the paradoxes of anxiety disorders is the need to sometimes accomplish tasks on the spur of the moment and at other times make elaborate plans in order to visualize being able to complete a task. For example, you may wake up one morning feeling relatively anxiety-free and spontaneously decide to go for a walk or a ride and happily head out the door. On the other hand, you may want to go to church and will have to plan out the entire scenario, such as sitting in the pew closest to the door and having your car parked right outside the church's

door for a fast escape. If you are expecting company you may plan on having a safe person on hand if you fear you might need to leave the room for a while to collect yourself. Creating these types of safeguards for ourselves can usually make completing a given task easier.

10. Change of any kind is hard for us; we love the predictable and familiar. Unfortunately, life doesn't usually work that way. While I love the teachings of Buddhism, I go kicking and screaming when I have to look at their concept of the impermanence of all things! I have been told that when I am at my worst, it is unwise to even try and wear a new blouse, as that subtle change might throw me into more anxiety. This came to the forefront even more decidedly during one of my interviews for the *Tampa Bay Times*, when I was asked how I chose what to wear each day. I realized that when I wore something even slightly unfamiliar when I had company, my anxiety increased. Now I simply wear comfortable clothing I am accustomed to when faced with a new situation.

11. It can be very difficult for us to make commitments because we never know how we are going to feel on any given day or even *minute* in the future. We can schedule an appointment on a day when we are feeling okay, only to have the appointed day arrive and wonder what we could have been thinking! We feel as if our body has betrayed us and we can become saddened and frustrated and feel like a failure. After having to cancel an event any number of times at the last minute, we may be deemed unfriendly, unreliable and/or not trustworthy. Please keep in mind that you can only do the best you can do; simply trying is a triumph! Just because it is hard to make a commitment doesn't mean you shouldn't make the attempt and try to follow through. In my case, the minute I get out of bed I do everything I can, like take out the garbage or put the outgoing mail in the mailbox, just in case I can't do it later. I'd like to point out here that some of our responses may be beyond our control. I know that I have tried *everything* I could to overcome this disorder without any permanent success. There are studies currently underway that show that people with agoraphobia may have

differences in the amygdala (fear response center) in their brains and therefore might have a biological factor contributing to their responses. Google it and you will find some interesting statistics!

12. During periods of severe anxiety, we might keep items we think we may need close by for fear we will freeze from the fear and be unable to retrieve them, especially at night or first thing in the morning. We may choose to have unperishable food, a cool washcloth in a zippie bag, bottled water, a book, the remote for the television, medications, and the telephone and phone numbers on or in the nightstand, and even a portable potty or bucket near the bed. We feel that we have to plan for any eventuality—just in case. We are good boy and girl scouts and think we always have to be prepared!

13. Another of the extra-added attractions of agoraphobia is *anticipatory anxiety*. This is not only becoming anxious or panic-stricken in the actual event, but *anticipating* how you are going to feel or react. This can bring on the same (or worse) high levels of anxiety as actually being in the situation. For example:

If you are socially phobic, the thought of someone being in your home is particularly uncomfortable for you. One stormy winter day your furnace cuts out. Now you have to call a repairman to come and fix it. The thought fills you with terror. Your mind begins to race: "What if it's something horribly wrong with the heater and I have to get it replaced and he'll be here for *days* and I will have to hand him tools and feed him dinner and put him up in my guest room and he'll like it here so much he'll *never* leave?" So now, before you even make the phone call, you're running around with your hair on fire and have yourself so juiced you'd rather freeze to death than have that repairman in your house. You finally work up the brave to make the call, and the repairman gets there, only to find it's simply the pilot light has gone out and it's a three-minute fix. So, you've spent an entire day panicked to the eyeballs, when in fact, the reality wasn't all that bad. You coped, got your pilot light lit and he left. End of story. But the *anticipatory anxiety* really had you going and made you miserable for the better part of that day.

14. Seeing a doctor can be problematic. Again, this is a paradox. We fear what the doctor might find and whether we can handle any possible negative outcomes, so we avoid seeking medical attention. Some of us, however, find comfort in seeing a doctor regularly to be reassured that all is well and what we are feeling is only anxiety. At this point in time, I will not have my blood pressure taken because I know the results will be high and I may be required to take medication that I might have a reaction to. This may sound like a dangerous proposition, but I also know that my high blood pressure is situational: a stranger of whom I am afraid is in my house, performing procedures of which I am afraid, therefore my blood pressure will be elevated. In this circumstance, there is no way a doctor can get an accurate reading. Medical attention can be challenging for sure! If you are currently receiving medical treatment in your home of any kind, i.e. doctor, dentist, optometrist, podiatrist, whatever, please pass that information along to me via email (eaisaksen@gmail.com). I am starting a section on my website, http://living-with-agoraphobia.com, containing a list of

medical professionals and all kinds of other services catering to those who are housebound. This is such valuable information for us with very little available to service the demand.

15. Many of us who suffer from anxiety disorders have a need to be hyper-organized. This stems from the lack of control inside, breeding the compulsion to be in control of things outside. This may even border on obsessive behavior.

16. Between the anticipatory anxiety (see item #13) and the feeling of our safe place being invaded, it may take us a long time—especially if we live alone—to do home repairs, such as replacing a faucet or having a new appliance installed. We would much rather put up with bad WiFi than risk a visit from the cable guy!

17. Personal hygiene can be a challenge for some, especially in regards to the shower. The claustrophobic feeling of confinement behind that closed shower curtain, the excessive steam giving you the sensation of having difficulty breathing and the trapped feeling once the shampoo/soap is applied can all bring about anxiety symptoms. If this

is an issue for you, try having someone (a person with whom you feel comfortable being naked!) in the house when you are in the shower. Leave the bathroom door open so you know they will be able to hear you if you call out. You can also leave the shower curtain open to lessen the feeling of confinement (don't worry about getting the floor wet... It's only water that can easily be mopped up later!) Open a window to allow the steam to escape. Keep the lighting to your personal taste. Some people like the room well-lit while people like me, prefer just a soft light. Play music or listen to an audio book if that is soothing to you. Invest in a shower chair. Having this handy little item may help enormously. If you are especially phobic about this, lessen your time in the shower by washing your hair at the sink and shaving the whatever-you-shave places prior to getting in.

18. Holiday gatherings, birthdays and other social events can be a nightmare as opposed to the joyous occasions they are meant to be because we view them as "have-to" instead of "want-to" occurrences. If you are socially phobic, this can be an even bigger challenge. If the circumstance

dictates that your attendance to one such event is mandatory, plan for it as much as possible. In these situations, a safe person is invaluable. If the affair is happening outside your home, have a trusted friend or family member go with you. Park as close to the building as is feasible, hang out near an exit, and excuse yourself to the restroom or other place away from the party so you can catch your breath and center yourself. If you are hosting the event, have your safe person available to step in to take over the hosting duties should you need to take a breather. You may find that having these safeguards in place will actually lower your anxiety and you may not need to employ them at all. Let's take a moment here to remind ourselves that these baby steps may only be necessary until such time as you become totally comfortable in these situations. Practice most certainly can make perfect!

19. Another classic symptom of agoraphobia is catastrophic or "what if" thinking. As I have said many times before, people with anxiety disorders are extremely intelligent, creative and imaginative people, but they allow those wonderful qualities to work against themselves. It is *because* you have that

incredible imagination that you can see every conceivable side to any given situation. For example: You are stopped at a traffic light, one car ahead of you, and a few behind you. You drum your fingers against the steering wheel, impatiently waiting for the light to turn green. Suddenly, the thought floats through your mind: "What if this light is broken and I am stuck here forever??? (Phobics are frequently absolute thinkers: There aren't many gray areas, just black and white. And everything is extreme, like "never," "forever," "always.") What if I have a heart attack and the ambulance can't reach me because of all these cars around me? What if the car in front of me breaks down and I can't get around him?" (You get my drift here.) Now, the three other non-phobic drivers stuck in that line of traffic are calmly distracting themselves by filing their nails, reading the paper, cleaning out the glove box and digging out the spare change from between the seats, while *you* are having a grand old time making yourself nuts by coming up with scenario after scenario, each one worse than the last. So you're off to the races again, adrenaline pumping merrily away.

20. Breathing can be a concern. Although I have no statistical data to support this, it has been my experience that it's about a 50-50 proposition between those of us who over-breathe (hyperventilate) and those who under-breathe (holding one's breath). Each issue can be solved by practicing slow, controlled breathing from the diaphragm. Simply place your hand, fingers splayed, on your abdomen with your thumb centered just below your pectoral muscles over your diaphragm. Breathe in slowly to a count of four, seeing your hand rise on your upper abdomen. Then breathe out slowly to a count of four, watching your hand resume its original position. Practice this several times per day for ten to fifteen minutes at a time and soon you will be able to control your breathing.

21. We are definitely not people who can be easily coerced or bribed into doing something. Some people think that if we just had a big enough payoff we'd get moving. I can tell you from very personal experience that is not true. Once I applied for disability and had to go into an attorney's office for an interview. This was at a time when I could go out minimally. The

office was only about two miles or so from where I was staying. A good friend drove me in her van to the appointment. About a mile into our journey I told her I had to go back. I was terrified and felt I could not ride for another moment. Since the distance was so short I did manage to get to the office, but could not go in. The attorney ended up coming out to the van and did the interview on the floor of the vehicle! In a couple of weeks I got a call from him stating that I had to go into the city (about 25 miles away) for a final interview. I just froze and told him that there was no way I could do that. I knew I was risking my disability, but felt powerless. I told him that if *I could* go into the city for that interview I wouldn't need the disability! I did not go.

22. We are usually people who have difficulty concentrating, especially during times of high anxiety, and prefer things that are brief and to-the-point. We may have a challenging time following someone who is telling a long and detailed description of an event. That is one reason for the relative brevity of this book.

Abovementioned are quite a few quirks we may have in common. While we are very sensitive, have a tendency to over-react and may have to occasionally reel in our thinking, we are also people who:

1. Have outgoing personalities and can be a lot of fun to be around

2. Are very creative and imaginative in the best of ways

3. Are very loving and loveable

4. Are very interesting

5. Are very intelligent and have very high potential

6. Are very ethical

So, it is important to know that we are so much more than our anxiety. The anxiety is just one small part of the whole that is you. Please always try to keep that in mind so you can continue to grow and to develop all the other facets of the amazing person that is you.

AVOIDANCE

The word *agoraphobia* technically means fear of open spaces; however, the essence of agoraphobia is a fear of panic attacks. If you suffer from agoraphobia, you are afraid of being in situations from which escape might be difficult-or in which help might be unavailable-if you suddenly had a panic attack. You may avoid grocery stores or freeways, for example, not so much because of their inherent characteristics, but because these are situations from which escape might be difficult or embarrassing in the event of panic. Fear of embarrassment plays a key role. Most agoraphobics fear not only having panic attacks but what other people will think should they be seen having a panic attack.

The Anxiety & Phobia Workbook, Edmund J. Bourne, Ph.D.

People with panic disorder often develop agoraphobia-the tendency to avoid places or situations where escape might be difficult or embarrassing or where help might be unavailable in the event of a panic attack. While the types of places or situations avoided vary greatly from person to person and sometimes even from time to time, a definite pattern is usually present. A person with this condition may need a companion, called a support person, when traveling away from home or into new or frightening areas. A support person ensures the availability of help. The agoraphobic avoidance can range from mild to severe.

Anxiety, Phobias & Panic, Reneau Z. Peurifoy, M.A., M.F.C.C.

Although avoidance might technically qualify as a quirk, it is common to all agoraphobics and important enough to rate a chapter of its own.

Let's set the scene:

You are in the grocery store squeezing melons and all of a sudden you feel a wave of dizziness wash over you. Your palms begin to sweat, your heart rate increases, and you become short of breath. You don't know what is causing this, but one thing is crystal clear: **You have to get out of there!** You leave your shopping cart, your coupons, your grocery list (and maybe even the kid you have sitting in the cart—Just kidding!) in the middle of the aisle and race out of the store. And it's not until you are on your way home that these symptoms begin to subside. Sometimes you'll feel brave enough to go back to the store, but as you approach those melons again the memory of what happened the last time invades your brain and the symptoms reoccur. So it's exit, stage right once more. The next time you need to go to the store, the memory of that horrible feeling becomes overwhelming, so you get your spouse/neighbor/relative to do the shopping for you. Thus begins the chain of avoidance...

Next scenario: You're standing in line at the bank, tapping your foot impatiently at the little old lady in front of you counting out 86 years' worth of pennies. You look around, check out the bank manager's new suit, stock up on deposit slips (and any other freebies sitting on the counter), look out the window. All of a sudden, the thought occurs to you that this little old lady could take a very long time to make her transactions and you could be **trapped in that line forever!!!** Instead of brushing the thought away with a "Naaa... never happen," you begin to obsess on the idea of being trapped. The dizziness, palpitations, sweating and shortness of breath begin again and the next thing you know, you're halfway home, driving 90 miles per hour, deposit slips fluttering in the breeze. You think, "I sure don't want *that* to happen again!" and the chain of avoidance continues.

So now there are two places you won't go...

Once this chain of avoidance begins, it snowballs until you find there is very little you are comfortable doing. Your "safety zone" or territory continues to shrink until even the *thought* of going too far from home can bring on the symptoms. And before you know it, you are reduced to the perimeters of your house. It is not uncommon for phobics to shrink their territory to the point of becoming uncomfortable by simply looking out a window (been there, done that!). Suddenly, all those tasks you took for granted, bringing in the mail, taking out the garbage, grabbing the Sunday paper off the front step, become Herculean in nature. And you simply can't.

Actually, it's not all that sudden. It takes a long time—even years—to become sensitized to the point of becoming housebound. But once that chain of avoidance begins, it is very difficult to stop it. Sometimes it is so subtle you don't even realize it *is* happening until you recognize how drastically your life has changed. So, my point here is to try your *best* to keep your life going, no matter how uncomfortable it may be!

Making it Work

This section deals with the nitty gritty about how I make my life work on a daily basis, while living with my challenge. I share this in the hopes that you might pick up a tip or trick that will make your life a little easier.

1. The first thing I would like to address is the ever-popular question of "How do you get your groceries?" Everyone asks me this question, as if it was one of the great mysteries of the life. I have consulted on two plays and one movie and in all the interviews this was the #1 question. It's not like there aren't people all over the place that you can hire to do errands for you! I found a wonderful way to deal with this issue that works for me today. I barter. I found a woman named Tammy on Craigslist and I make her

shirts or other advertising items for her business in exchange for doing my grocery shopping. Bartering is a great way to do business and a lost art. I have also managed to make a good friend in the process!

2. For those of us who are housebound, even a simple thing like getting a haircut can prove to be daunting. My solution to that problem is using the Flowbee I purchased in 1981. It's the greatest gadget for cutting hair and saves me a lot of money as well as solves my hair cutting problems. Of course if you feel you can go out and get your hair done, by all means go, but if you cannot, this is a great solution. This also works for the elderly and those recovering from a hospital stay. There are also hairdressers that will come to your home. Check with nursing homes and trade schools to see if this is an option that will work for you.

Just about any type of shopping and banking can be done online. God bless computers and my friend Luci for convincing me to get one many years ago! When I find something that fits me from an online retailer like Walmart, such as jeans or shoes, I usually buy more than one pair. For most everything else, I use eBay or amazon.com. I don't have enough good things to say about amazon.com, especially their Prime plan which includes second day delivery.

3. Getting medical care can be a challenge if you are housebound. I have had to forego this in the past due to lack of availability. However, recently I was lucky enough to have found a visiting physician's service that makes house calls. I also had a dentist at one point, but unfortunately no longer do. I hope to rectify this situation in the future. One way to locate medical services that make home visits is to contact your local nursing homes. Sometimes doctors who have privileges there will make house calls in the nearby vicinity. Another good resource is Google.

I'd like to mention here again that if you currently have any of these types of services in place, please contact me through my website at http://living-with-agoraphobia.com so I can add it to the list.

4. To help me keep a handle on my day-to-day anxiety I presently have two counselors that I consult. I see David in my home regularly, which helps keep me on an even keel with the daily happenings in my life. I also have

occasional telephone sessions with Flora, who has been with me for many years. Flora is an agoraphobic specialist and can usually help me through a difficult time in a heartbeat. Both bring different and invaluable things to my life. Ongoing support is so important for anyone with our challenge in life. It has become easier to find a therapist who will do telephone sessions; however, medical insurance does not always cover this type of care.

5. If you don't have or can't afford a counselor, close friends or family members who can lend an ear can be a valuable resource. I have friends whom I have never met in person that I consider family! Luci is one such person. She is also a homebound agoraphobic and is the one person in my life that I can most identify with and who can identify with me. We have known each other for over 25 years and I am very fortunate to have her as a friend. We understand each other extremely well, as we are both dealing with the same challenges of being agoraphobic. It's very important to maintain friendships even if you cannot always get to see that person in person. Talk to your friends about how you feel, and ask them for help when necessary.

Opening up about how you feel is a huge key to reducing anxiety. If you are experiencing the so-called "negative" emotions, such as grief or anger, allow yourself to *feel* those feelings (And by the way, feelings are neither good or bad... they just *are*!). We need to fully experience *all* our emotions, not just the pleasant ones. Yes, it would be nice to feel happy all the time, but the reality is that grief, anger, pain and frustration are all part of the package. By the same token, no one is sad all the time either, so make a point to balance your conversations with friends and loved ones with lighter topics as well so they do not begin to feel overwhelmed or burdened.

6. If you are socially phobic and have difficulty cultivating new relationships, try telling the person a bit about yourself and the challenges you face bringing new people into your life. Setting boundaries is also a good idea. Let the person know that you need to proceed at a pace which is comfortable for you, and that you may need to initially see him or her for only short periods of time. Another way to help you become comfortable with a new person is to plan an activity or project you both enjoy

and can do together. You might try gardening, preparing a meal, learning/teaching a new craft, anything that keeps you active and engaged and allows your mind to stay busy. This will take the focus off you—and the anxiety—and allow the two of you to enjoy the time you spend together.

7. The telephone can be your best friend. I have learned to use this mode of communication to accomplish just about anything I could do in person. Sometimes I have had to get assertive or creative but I am usually successful in getting what I want and need. When my mom was ill and living with me, my house was like command central. I covered all her needs right from my home. Sometimes I'd even arrange teleconferencing with her doctors and health care providers to straighten out certain situations! Other issues like tending to bill problems can be dealt with via phone especially if you tell people you are disabled. I dislike using that word, but often it gets people's attention as well as their cooperation.

8. Maintaining a healthy diet is important. I try to eat fairly well. I eat a good breakfast, my

main meal at noon and a snack for dinner. By now many of you know that stimulants such as sugar, chocolate, nicotine and caffeine can be bad for us. There are many healthy diets out there but what I want to emphasize is that anxiety can wreak havoc with blood sugar levels. During times of high anxiety it is important to eat foods high in protein whenever possible. If you are planning an outing, take along something like cheese, hard-boiled eggs, cooked chicken or peanut butter. If you feel weak or light headed it can be from low blood sugar due to the anxiety. Protein is a healthy way to bring your blood sugar back to a normal level.

9. The other side of the diet coin is exercise. Maintaining a regular exercise regimen will not only promote a state of general health and well-being, but will also serve to dissipate the excessive adrenaline built up in your muscles that occurs during times of high anxiety levels. This does not mean you have to go out and spend a gozillion dollars on a home gym! Walking is one the cheapest, easiest and most effective forms of exercise you can use. If you are able to get outside, walk as far as you can, a few

houses up the street or even just up and down your driveway. If you cannot leave your house, a treadmill or exercise bike will do the trick. There are a multitude of exercise videos available; you can easily find something that appeals to you. Yoga, Pilates, and Zumba are a few examples. Dancing is also a wonderful and creative form of exercise. Do not choose a form of exercise that is beyond your physical capabilities; you need a plan you can stick to. If you are not used to being physically active, start small with five or ten minute sessions three times per week. You can increase this as your strength and stamina build. 20 – 30 minutes five times a week is a safe and healthy goal. Also keep in mind that physical exertion is the best way to dispel accumulated adrenaline. When you are very anxious, try to do something physical to facilitate this process. If you feel too anxious to get up and move, simply sit and tense and relax individual muscle groups. This will expedite the process of getting your adrenaline back to normal levels.

10. Staying creative is a wonderful way to distract yourself from your anxiety. Try to get

up every day with the thought of something interesting that you can do or become involved in. This has helped me enormously. It may take a little time to decide what form of creativity appeals to you, but if you focus on the things you *can* do it will give you more reason to be joyful in your day. Whatever it is, stay as positive as you can and try to have *fun* with what you choose to do. The important thing is to try to get out of your own head a little and stay involved in the world, even from home. I have a business making custom printed items and I often get very excited when I think about a new design I can create. My friend Luci crochets like she is demonically possessed, making afghans for her friends and family as well as hats and scarves for children in a local daycare. You might choose to learn a new skill, such as speaking a foreign language, painting, writing poetry, cooking a different cuisine, or playing a musical instrument. You may also choose to become more proficient in a skill you already possess. In this age of the Internet, there are a myriad of ways to accomplish these things right from home.

11. *Ac-cen-tu-ate the positive, e-li-minate the negative* is how the old song goes. Keep

positive thoughts in your head as much as possible to reduce the racing thoughts that plague most of us. One thing that helps me is listening to interesting or inspirational audiobooks. Since I am usually very busy on a daily basis running my home-based business and attending to the necessary daily activities of my life, I rarely have time to sit down and read a book from cover to cover. I joined audible.com (a division of amazon.com) and can now "read" while I am working or doing household chores. I find that even if I don't hear every word of a book some of the messages get through. Many times when my mind decides to run amok, I can concentrate on the words from the book instead of random scary or negative thoughts. This practice gives the brain an alternate and positive place to focus. You can find some book recommendations in the last section of this book as well as on my website.

12. Having a routine is very important for me. It helps keep me organized and less scattered, which is something I don't do well with. It's good to break from your routine once in a while so you don't become rigid, but for me a daily routine helps to keep my anxiety

down. However, don't make the mistake of cramming your day so full of tasks and activities that you feel overwhelmed. It is never necessary to complete your whole list in one day. Prioritize and keep the rest for the next day. Once again small increments and baby steps are the way to go!

13. To quote a favorite movie, "Don't forget: You have to have a little fun every day." Laughter is so healing. Find something humorous to laugh about every day, even if you are the butt of the joke. Some of my funniest stories pertain to my agoraphobia. One of them is about a parrot I had at one time named Crackers. Once I went to put him in his cage and was very anxious and not focusing and tried to stuff him in the garbage can. Another time I tried to stuff him in the microwave! Poor Crackers! I hope your stories are less threatening to your pets! Incidentally, pets can be a calming influence as well as a source of laughter and fun. Their unconditional love is invaluable. I am an animal lover and have owned everything from horses and sheep to monkeys and reptiles. Today I just have two dogs and a parrot named Graycie.

14. As the song goes, "Take it easy, take it easy. Don't let the sound of your own wheels drive you crazy." As a group, agoraphobics are people who are easily stimulated and therefore tend to move quickly and have racing thoughts during times of increased anxiety. I have noticed that if I slow *everything* down—walking, talking, movement in general—usually my thoughts will follow. Again, this takes practice. My friend Luci has used this technique by tracing the words she is saying with her finger on a flat surface, very slowly, one letter at a time. She uses phrases such as "Take it down," "Take it easy," "There is no hurry," to calm her mind. If you have an appointment, plan ahead to make sure you allow yourself plenty of time to get ready and get to it. Move slowly, talk to yourself slowly, slowly, s-l-o-w-l-y.

15. Getting the proper amount of sleep is *vital*. I cannot stress this enough. I find an enormous difference in myself when I do not get adequate sleep. I am pretty rigid these days about my sleep habits. My days start very early in the morning, so I make them end early. No matter how busy I am during the day, this is non-negotiable. I go

into my bedroom soon after dinner and just rest. I might watch a little mindless television, read, or listen to music. I always meditate before retiring to compose my body and calm my mind and spirit to facilitate a good night's sleep. I do my best to bring my day to a peaceful end by giving myself enough time to unwind before going to sleep. I have found that following this routine really makes a difference.

16. I have found meditation to be invaluable. Merriam-Webster.com defines the word *meditate* as either of the following:

    A. to engage in contemplation or reflection

    B. to engage in mental exercise (as concentration on one's breathing or repetition of a mantra) for the purpose of reaching a heightened level of spiritual awareness

    It is important to realize that some of the most basic things can be considered to be meditation. Simply looking at a beautiful sky and thinking peaceful thoughts or playing soft, soul-moving music are considered meditative. Many people today are into more structured forms of mediation. Some are meant to relax us and some are meant to create altered states of consciousness. Today, Mindfulness Meditation is one of the most popular methods. Mindfulness is unique in that it does not attempt to have us be any different than how we are. Instead, it tries to get us to simply get closely in touch with who and how we are in any given place in time. It helps us to live in the present moment, no matter what that moment is and guides us to accept our lives as is and coexist with whatever thoughts, feelings and situations truly exist for us at that moment. Following/focusing on your breath is a wonderful way to tune out all other thoughts and just be with who you are. Doing this for even short periods of time can calm the body and mind enormously. One great thing to meditate on is the person you really are deep within, the one without the anxiety. We all have that part. If we can get in touch with other parts of ourselves, the parts we truly love and remember from days when we didn't have anxiety, it gives us hope that we can be that way again. That person in not gone, just a bit covered up!

17. I try to remain as honest as I possibly can about my challenge with anxiety and am open with others about it. This was not

always the case. There was a time when I used to be embarrassed about my condition and would make a multitude of excuses as to why I couldn't do the things others wanted me to do. These days I no longer focus much on what people may think about me or the unique way I live. This is my life and I have to live it as best I can. Since my anxiety is rarely obvious simply by looking at me, I have to share how I am feeling with others so they will know. You may be hesitant to try this at first, but believe me, it is far easier in the long run to be open and honest about your condition rather than to keep trying to hide it. Don't expect the non-phobic population to understand what you are dealing with. This is one of these situations where understanding is reached only by experience. The best you can hope for is that the people around you accept that *you* understand your condition, and are doing the very best you can every day. I ask people to simply work with me to try to make some things doable. Those who are willing to do so are invariably kept in my life longer.

Ours is an invisible illness, one of the most difficult to deal with because it is not obvious. If we had no legs no one would expect us to dance, but when there is nothing visibly wrong with us others may have expectations that are beyond our capabilities. It is vital that you trust yourself to know that you are truly doing the best you can. That's all you can do, so do not fall into the trap of beating yourself up just because you have a few limitations that most other people cannot see or understand. There are many people in this world who are more than willing to go the extra mile to love and support you. It's just a matter of finding them and cultivating that relationship. When you do find them, you must do your best to trust, to let the love and caring in so you can have as much support as possible to go forward on your journey.

It is my wish for all of us that others would see beyond the fear and into our hearts to the real being inside. We are so much more than just anxiety!

SYSTEMATIC
DESENSITIZATION

In this section I will be discussing an important method used to help overcome anxiety reactions. I have used this technique with success in many situations. This process is called *Systematic Desensitization* and was developed by Dr. Arthur Hardy. It is explained in depth in the TERRAP manual as found below. First, let's examine the term sensitization and what it means in psychological terms.

In this sense, sensitization is the process of becoming highly sensitive to specific events or situations (especially emotional events or situations). For agoraphobics, there can be a highly charged emotional reaction to many life events. Most, but not all, of these reactions pertain to trying to do things that are outside of our comfort zone, such as going to the grocery store or driving. We could call these types of situations territorial. However, these reactions can also happen in relation to situations that can happen within our comfort zone, such as having an unfamiliar visitor in our home. This might fall into the category of social phobia. Agoraphobia may encompass several different types of phobias. No matter what the trigger, however, systematically trying to desensitize to whatever the stimulus is can be very helpful.

A medical example of sensitization is allergies. First, one can be allergic to something he or she is unaware of. The allergy specialist first determines, by testing, what is causing the sensitivity. Secondly, a person may be so overly sensitive that even the smallest amount of material will cause a severe reaction. The third similarity is that the treatment requires diluting the sensitizing material down to a level where it can be injected and only a mild reaction occurs. Then, by frequent injections the dosages are gradually increased, and by allowing the individual to recover fully before the next injection, desensitization takes place. By proceeding on a regular basis over a period of time, the person builds up a greater tolerance for the allergen and finally arrives at a place whereby exposure to the full strength material produces a tolerable reaction or no allergic reaction at all.

Now let's translate this into phobias. We might say that the phobic person has become allergic [supersensitive] to certain emotional stimuli. When exposed to that stimulus he or she overreacts both emotionally and physiologically. If you have phobias, and the anxiety reactions that go with them, you first have to identify the specific stimuli that touch off the super reaction. Once you have identified a noxious or triggering stimulus, you can then expose yourself to that stimulus in small doses on a regular basis in gradually increasing amounts until a tolerance is developed to full strength exposure to that stimulus. It's like taking baby steps out of your comfort zone and trying to accomplish doing a new or difficult task an inch at a time.

Now how do you discover what your triggering stimuli are? One way is to write down everything you can think of which causes you any problem at all. You can do this over a period of time, perhaps a week. During that week, you write down anything and everything that occurs to you at the time the reaction is occurring.

Next, arrange the list from the least troublesome fear to the most troublesome fear. This will be your hierarchy of fears.

The goal in desensitization is this: When there is a stimulus that triggers anxiety, you need to get to the point where that stimulus loses its capacity to cause you anxiety, so that in the presence of that stimulus you can remain relaxed.

Basically, the desensitization process for phobias is composed of three parts: imaginal desensitization, visual desensitization, and in-vivo or "real life" desensitization. You must always start with imaginal desensitization, since our first area of avoidance is always in our minds.

Imaginal desensitization:

Start with your least bothersome fear.

1. Imagine that you are in the situation that causes anxiety and stay there in your imagination until you react to a point where you are just slightly uncomfortable (a #3 on the anxiety scale). Do not picture yourself experiencing any anxiety at all in the situation; instead picture yourself dealing with it the way you would like to feel.

2. In your mind, retreat from the situation, distract your mind and go to your safe place in your imagination.

3. Allow yourself to relax completely.

4. Wait, relaxed, until you are completely recovered. If feelings are stirred up, allow yourself to feel them. Often strong feelings

will begin to emerge as you go through this process, but do NOT run from them. This is a good sign that progress is being made.

5. Repeat the process over again.

Keep repeating this process until the stimulus in the situation you have chosen to think about causes very little or no anxiety when you think about it.

These steps are called the five R's and they are very important:

> React
> Retreat
> Relax
> Recover
> Repeat

Many people report that they cannot seem to arouse any anxiety when they are just thinking about a stimulus. That is fine!

You may feel tempted to skip this first step in the desensitization process. Do not fall into this trap! You do not have to feel any anxiety in order for imaginal desensitization to work. The key is in the repetition and frequency; the more frequently you practice imaginal desensitization, the better the transference to the real-life situation. The imaginal desensitization process is vital to your recovery. Always start with it whether it arouses your anxiety or not.

Visual desensitization:

Using the same stimulus, the next step is to use visual stimulation in the form of pictures. See if you can find photos of the situation/ person that triggers you: A photo of a grocery store, family gathering, cars on the freeway etc...

1. Look at the picture until you react only to a #3 anxiety level.

2. Retreat: walk away from the picture, back off from it or turn it over, and distract your mind.

3. Relax.

4. Allow yourself to recover completely. If feelings are stirred up, again allow yourself to feel them.

5. Repeat the process until looking at the picture causes very little or no anxiety.

Now you are ready for the last step: approaching the situation in- vivo (real life). I want to stress here that you do not start this step until you have progressed through the first two steps in the desensitization process. After you have completed these two steps using the same stimulus, then you are ready to try in- vivo desensitization.

In- vivo desensitization:

During this phase of the desensitization process,

it would be very helpful if you can engage the assistance of a supportive person. This would be someone who can actively participate in what you are trying to accomplish. The added support and encouragement is invaluable.

Using the same stimulus as in the two previous steps, approach the situation with no specific goal in mind. For example, if you are attempting to get to the grocery store, do not do so with the intention of making any purchases. Your goal is to desensitize yourself, not buy groceries. It is very important that you make a clear distinction between practice and demand situations. A demand situation would be one where you were out of bread and *had* to go to the grocery store. Again the process entails the Five R's:

> React
> Retreat
> Relax
> Recover
> Repeat

1. Approach the situation until you react only up to a #3 anxiety level.

2. Retreat: Stop, back off, turn around, take a few steps toward the door or walk away.

3. Distract your mind and allow yourself to relax.

4. Wait until you are completely recovered and allow yourself to express any feelings that have been stirred up.

5. Return to the situation and repeat the process.

There are a few points here that need to be emphasized:

1. Do not let your anxiety rise above a #3 before you retreat. You are training yourself to respond to this situation in a calm fashion, and allowing your anxiety levels to rise above a #3 will only reinforce the fear.

2. Retreat is not cowardly; it is vital. Retreat and regroup just as they do in the military; that's how wars are won. Retreat does not mean that you have to leave the situation or run away. You may only need to stop where you are and back off a few paces, or go to another room for a few minutes. If you can't actually leave the situation, even for a few minutes, you can also retreat by going to a safe, calm scene/place in your mind until you get used to the situation. Remember, you are not retreating forever; just until you recover.

   Retreat seems to be a very difficult concept for people to think about, let alone do.

Thoughts and comments such as "I'll feel like a coward," or "People will think it's funny or something's wrong with me," often keep one from practicing retreating. This is no time to worry about what other people will think! You want to recover, and in order to do so you need to learn how to desensitize yourself, which means you *must* practice this process. Retreat is a necessary and vital part of the desensitization process. Practice retreating as much as you can.

3. You must keep repeating the desensitiza-tion process (all three steps) in order for it to work. You'll find as you keep repeating it, that you are able to approach closer and stay longer in the situation.

4. If you are having a particularly difficult time in your life due to stress caused by family discord, divorce. a loss or just ongoing arguments with a loved one, you may want to put your practice on hold for a short while. Emotional distress can adversely affect your practice.

The desensitization process that I have just described is a natural process. If left to our own devices, and if we were not worried about what other people think, we would automatically use this process when we approached anything new. For instance, a small child goes to the beach for the first time and sees the ocean. He or she does not plunge into the water, but cautiously approaches it. The child looks at it from a distance and then, as his or her courage grows, gets closer. Each time he or she gets closer, courage grows and fears diminish. Eventually he or she will gradually stick a foot into the water, then a leg, then his or her body and arms. Notice, however, that the child has been left to his or her own devices. If, on the other hand, the child has been overly cautioned by his or her mother about the dangers of the water, he or she will start to worry about Mom's approval, be frightened by the dangers she suggested, become sensitized and will probably not approach the water. This could spread to all water, so that the child will become panicky at the thought of taking a bath. At this point, instead of the natural desensitization process, the child will have to begin to consciously practice desensitizing him or herself to the water.

Because you have become sensitized to some stimuli and situations, you need to start practicing desensitizing yourself. I hope this method proves to be helpful to you. It takes time and may require the cooperation of some of the people around you, but the payoff can be amazing!

THE TOOLBOX

In this section, I will be discussing my toolbox. Not the literal bulky metal container that holds a hammer and screwdriver, but the figurative toolbox containing a list of "go to" things to do when I am especially stressed or anxious. Again, some items are redundant, but they bear repeating.

It has been my experience that everyone—even those who seem to have it all together—has some cross to bear or some mountain to climb in this life. It is helpful—and wise—to have at our disposal a collection of things (tools) that can help us cope in difficult and stressful situations. It may take some time and much trial and error to discover what will work for you. You may also find that something that worked yesterday may not work today. This is why it is a good idea to have a large assortment of aids from which to choose. Over the years I have built a fairly large collection of helpful tools. As you begin to fill your toolbox, make sure to write everything down! During times of stress or high anxiety you will be hard put to even remember what your tools are, let alone how to use them. Some of the things that may help me when I am very stressed or anxious are:

1. **Breathing Exercises**: I have found that using some simple breathing exercises will slow my body (heart rate) and mind (racing/catastrophic thoughts) down. I find that I think more clearly and often the anxiety will subside after only a ten or fifteen minute session. The simplest exercise is just to breathe in and out slowly to a count of four. Do this evenly for as long as it takes to get you into a better place. This works especially well if you are hyperventilating. You may be thinking, "This is ridiculous! I already know how to breathe!" Well, of course you do, but chances are you are breathing incorrectly. During times of stress or heightened anxiety, our breathing tends to become rapid, shallow and high up in the chest. By practicing the deeper breathing repeatedly, you will be able to revert to it when needed simply by saying to yourself: "Breathe." It will eventually become an automatic response. There are many more elaborate exercises available on the internet

that might work for you. For example, I have recently started doing something called "alternate nostril breathing" that helps me enormously to get a rested night's sleep. I also have an app for my IPad called "Breathing Zone" that can work wonders. Search around on the internet and see if any of the exercises appeal to you.

2. **Positive Self-Talk:** Your mind cannot differentiate between thoughts and actions, which is why imagery works so well. When we have catastrophic thoughts, we believe them to be the reality, even if that is far from the case. What we believe to be true is. Everyone is wired this way, not just those of us with anxiety disorders. If you tell yourself something terrible is about to happen, you *will* believe it and react accordingly. This is one of the reasons that we may often have the need to be comforted and reassured by others. When we become panicky, we may not trust ourselves enough to know that we are all right; we may even desperately need the calming input of another person to reassure us that we will survive this episode and that we are, in fact, really okay. The truth is, it is what *we* tell ourselves that truly matters. It is *our* beliefs that affect us. When we learn to calm ourselves down we have a tool that will always

be available to us! My friend Luci used to look to her mother for reassurance when she was especially anxious. She would wait for her mom to smile and only then would she feel relief. She knew that if her mother was smiling, she had to be okay. She eventually figured out that she could achieve the same effect if she smiled at herself in a mirror. Along the same lines, if we tell ourselves that we cannot ever be a whole person if we are unable to comfortably leave our homes then that will be our reality. If, on the other hand, we decide not to buy into what society deems "normal" and focus on what we CAN do on any given day, our whole perspective about who we are can change. It is my belief that who we are as people (our inner life) is much more important than what we do or how far we can travel (our outer life). Consequently, if it be true that one's inner life is at least as important (if not more important) than one's outer life, you can be a whole person without ever leaving your house! So, try different perspectives and see how talking lovingly and supportively to yourself can make a difference in how you feel and view your world.

Two more thoughts on self-talk: First, you must be honest with yourself. If you are in the throes of a panic attack, telling yourself "I feel GREAT!" isn't going to cut it. It may be a great thought, but it is probably not something you will buy. Instead, say something like, "This sucks, but I can handle it." Stay real in your self-talk; your mind and body know the truth! Next, your positive self-talk must be... well... POSITIVE! You are trying to erase those old negative tapes with something better. Affirmations are a great way to accomplish this. Keep them short, keep them simple and keep them upbeat! Create your own; start out with just one or two repeated frequently throughout the day. Write them on the bathroom mirror, leave yourself sticky notes all over the house—whatever it takes to keep those good thoughts in the forefront. Add more as time goes on. Examples of a few simple affirmations are "I am safe," "I am loved," "I am strong," "I am a viable human being." You get the drift here. Use what works for you.

3. **Put Your Anxiety in the Background:** I can hear the laughter now. I realize that this seems impossible—and sometimes it is. What I am suggesting is that you try not to have your anxiety be the focus of your every waking moment and that you learn to peacefully coexist with it. I am stating very clearly that there is a full life beyond your anxiety if you

only give it a chance to develop. For decades I got up, put the key in the car and focused only on if I could drive around the block that day. If I couldn't—and I often couldn't—I felt like a failure. The disappointment coupled with the exhaustion of the energy spent (anxiety can be *very* exhausting!) left me depleted and without much interest in the rest of my day. Then I began just waking up and focusing on what I really wanted to do. If that included going out, fine and if it didn't that was fine too. As a result I ended up developing my creativity (as I mentioned before, most agoraphobics are very intelligent and creative) and found myself developing a home-based business and writing and doing all kinds of fun things. My focal point was *not* on anxiety; it was on building my life to be the best it could be with what I had to work with.

4. **Acceptance:** *Acceptance is arguably the most important tool in my toolbox!* It was a word I learned years ago from Dr. Claire Weekes, a pioneer in the study and treatment of agoraphobia. She continually suggested that acceptance was the key to dealing with this condition. Instead of getting up every day hoping and praying that the anxiety is gone, or perhaps more to the point, fearing that is not,

just accept *what is* on that particular day. If you stop fighting it, life can be much more peaceful and you will find you have much more energy to accomplish the things you really want to tackle. Acceptance is not the same as giving up. Acceptance simply means that you are willing to roll with whatever comes up that day or however you feel. Promise yourself you will do your best each day to achieve what you can and be the best person you can. Then just let the rest fall where it may!

5. **Journaling:** Another invaluable tool to employ on a daily basis is keeping a journal. This can be an extremely cathartic process. The benefits to journaling are threefold: First, this gives you a completely private place to vent your true feelings. Your journal is just that: YOURS! No one else will be reading it, so you have free license to write whatever you would like. This is a stellar opportunity to do a little daily housecleaning of your mind, getting rid of the excess emotional baggage you accumulated during that day. Second, journaling allows you to chart the progress you are making in your recovery. You can keep track of any practices you may have done that day, how you felt while you were doing them and whether or not you deemed them successful (remember-just *trying* is a

success!). Third, over time you will be able to see patterns in your behavior, both good and bad. For example, if you were to look back over the past 30 days in your journal and notice that every time you came in contact with a specific person or situation you became anxious, this would demonstrate a pattern. You would then know this is an area you have to work on to determine why that person or scenario triggered the anxiety and what you can do to remedy the situation.

You don't have to write *War and Peace* every time you sit down with your journal. Some days a simple sentence, such as "Feeling the same as yesterday" will suffice. Other days, you may feel compelled to write pages and pages. This is a matter of quality, not quantity. The medium in which you keep your journal doesn't matter either. You might feel more comfortable using the word processing program on your computer, or you may opt to write longhand with paper and pencil. Nor does it matter what time of day you choose to write, although it can be very beneficial to do your journaling shortly before going to bed. This serves to clear your mind of those pesky thoughts that keep you awake, allowing you to get a better night's sleep.

6. **Distractions:** Distracting yourself from the anxiety that you are experiencing in the present moment can be extremely helpful. Sometimes I can get lost in my work, especially if I am involved in a creative project. I try to find something that requires a lot of concentration and see if I can redirect my attention and energy there. I love electronic gadgets so if I have something that needs figuring out I often will do that at those times. Of course there are times when the anxiety is just so high it is very hard to concentrate on much of anything. At those times, tackle something simpler, like cleaning out the junk drawer or playing some computer solitaire. Just trying to walk it off or do some form of exercise might help as well.

A funny story about distraction centers on an attempt I once made to visit a mall with a good friend. I got there okay and was about a quarter of the way in when I started to panic. My friend recognized the look on my face and decided to distract me. She was a funny character who could usually make me laugh. On this occasion she grabbed me by the scruff of the neck, turned me around and headed me toward the exit. As we walked, she stopped me at *each* store window on the way out and made me peruse the merchandise displayed. She told me if I didn't calm down, she was going to drag me into the store to fill out a job application. I laughed so hard I almost forgot I was so panicky. I *did* get back to the car and I *did* survive.

7. **Meditation/Relaxation:** I cannot emphasize the importance of practicing some form of meditation or relaxation technique enough. Learning to bring our bodies and minds down to a low level of excitation is vital. Although it may seem as if meditation is a new craze, it has, in fact, been in practice since at least 500 B.C. in the Eastern religions. Many people claim that they simply cannot sit still and shut down their minds no matter how hard they try. However, meditation can take many forms. You can look into traditional methods and various yoga practices, but simply being with nature or listening to soothing, soul-touching music can be meditative. Holding your pet close and just cuddling for a while can have similar results. Keep trying different things to see what works for you.

Sometimes while meditating if I try to focus on and draw forward my "inner Ellen," the one who is loving and peaceful that I remember from my days in college, I relax. I am in touch with the authentic me, the one that is stifled by the anxiety. Anxiety truly suffocates creativity and our real, loving being. Try to get in touch with your own by visualizing and calling forth the person you remember yourself to be without the anxiety. Visualization can be very powerful; truly KNOW and BELIEVE that person is still in there, because he/she truly is.

8. **Humor:** A little humor goes a long way. Try to find something funny to laugh at every day. I have another very humorous story centering around my anxiety disorder. One day, while I was still able to venture out to some degree, I decided to mosey up to the corner to take a peek at the new CVS pharmacy that was having a grand opening on that day. I managed to get a parking spot directly in front of the door so I decided to venture out of my car and take a *quick* look inside the new building. The store looked somewhat inviting and since my anxiety level was not all that high, I tentatively put a foot into the store. I noticed that they had greeting cards next to the cash registers right in the front of the store so I decided to get even braver and see if I could purchase one. It had been a long time since I was actually able to pick out a special card for someone and send it.

I looked briefly at the cards in front of me and finally proceeded to make a purchase. I headed over to the cashier and noticed that no one else was there. I was delighted, thinking I could make a very quick exit and be in my car in a nanosecond. WRONG! As I finished making my payment all kinds of bells and whistles went off and people started gathering around me!!! I was, in fact, the very FIRST customer in that new store and they were determined to make a big deal out of it. They directed me to go to the counter where they processed photos as they wanted to take my picture for the local newspaper! My heart was racing and I had ALL the classic symptoms of a juicy panic attack. Gasping for air, I told them I *had* to leave, but they were hearing none of it! Somehow, in a semiconscious stupor I ended up at that photo counter with light bulbs going off all over the place!! They were finally satisfied and I bolted out the door and fell into my car. I was frazzled, but laughing heartily to myself on the inside. I laughed even harder when I got home and realized that I had on a t-shirt that was less than desirable for a newspaper photograph! My friends saw the photo when the paper finally came out the following week and I have never been able to live down that story to this day. It is a lasting memory and always makes me laugh when I think about it. This could only happen to a poor, struggling agoraphobic who was trying to practice desensitization! I did, however, survive.

9. **Diet:** I'll keep this simple: Eating high protein foods can help regulate your blood sugar. Avoid caffeine, sugar and other stimulants when possible, as stimulants are usually the last thing we need.

10. I keep a cane close at hand for those occasions when I am experiencing higher levels of anxiety. I use it to balance myself when my legs feel like jelly or when I feel a little light headed, especially when going outside.

11. During periods of severe anxiety I keep items I think I might need (especially at night) close by. These might include unperishable food, a cool washcloth in a zippie bag, bottled water, a book, the remote for the television, medications, and the telephone and phone numbers on or in the nightstand, and even a portable potty or bucket near the bed. It can be comforting to know we can take care of ourselves should we feel immobilized by anxiety.

12. I use headphones to distract myself in certain situations such as cutting the lawn or even

talking to people if very nervous. In the latter situation I keep the volume down very low so I can hear the person, yet have the music quietly running in the background. If you explain to people why you are doing this in their presence they will not be offended. Music or audiobooks can be a wonderful diversion during those times when we need to get the focus off of our anxiety. If you are not too anxious to read, try reading inspirational books. The messages or parables in the books are far better to focus on than scary thoughts.

13. Think creatively. Use your computer, iPad or some other resource to get the focus off the anxiety.

14. Plan ahead. For example: Stock your freezer with made-ahead meals to eliminate the pressure to perform every evening. Don't rush; allow ample time for each task at hand.

15. Take baby steps in all that you want to accomplish, especially new things. Try not to focus on what you believe other people are thinking about how you are meeting those challenges.

16. Call a friend or counselor. I use this tool quite often and consider myself blessed to have a few good friends who really get me, with whom

there is no need for lengthy explanations. It is a great release and a way to get a new and better perspective in many situations.

17. The last tool that I am going to mention here is something called the ABCD Principle (sometimes referred to as the ABCDE Principle). This was developed by Dr. Albert Ellis, founder of Rational Emotive Behavioral Therapy (REBT). This is a tool that can be extremely helpful in dealing with our negative or catastrophic thinking process. We create so much misery for ourselves with negative thinking and anticipatory anxiety. With this method, we can effectively challenge those thoughts. I have used it innumerable times with amazing results.

The theory is a simple one: Basically, you are defying those negative, unrealistic thoughts by countering them with more positive, accurate ones. In order to accomplish this, you must break it down.

A. The "A" stands for the *activating event* that has triggered your anxiety, i.e. "I am stuck in line at the grocery store. I feel trapped and am getting very anxious and panicky."

B. The "B" stands for the *belief* about the triggering event, i.e. "If I cannot quickly pass through this line I will get so anxious everyone will notice and think I am weird" or "I will get so anxious I will pass out or have a heart attack and make a scene and they will have to take me away by ambulance" or "If I get too anxious I will go crazy and they will take me away and lock me up!"

C. The "C" stands for the *consequences of the belief*, i.e. "I am so scared and NEVER want that to happen again so I will have to take someone with me next time so I can run away if I have to" or "I am so angry at myself for not being able to do such a simple thing and NEVER want that to happen again so I will NEVER go back to that store!" or "I feel so depressed and like a failure because I cannot be like everyone else. I will NEVER be able to do this or be normal."

D. The "D" stands for the *dispute* of the consequences, i.e. "The line in the store may seem slow, but if I wait here patiently it will move momentarily and I will be able to move on. No one is looking at me and I will not have a heart attack; I am simply anxious, and anxiety cannot hurt me. I am not now, nor have I ever been, crazy!" Think of the "D" as your sweet, calm voice of reason;

speak to yourself here as if you are addressing a beloved friend or family member.

Okay, you now have a feel for the principle. You can now create cards on which you will write down the entire ABCD for one specific scenario. Although index cards are suggested, a legal pad is just fine. Below is a sample of a completed ABCD card using the above scenario.

A Activating Event	I am stuck in a long line in the supermarket. I feel trapped and am getting very anxious.
B Belief	If I get too anxious people with look at me and think I am weird, or worse yet, I might pass out or have a heart attack or go crazy! If I get taken to the hospital I will surely die from fright!
C Consequence	I am so scared, angry and depressed. I am a worthless human being who can't even do a simple thing like my weekly shopping. I will NEVER go to that store again!

D Dispute	I have been in long lines many times before and sometimes gotten anxious, but I have NEVER fainted, had a heart attack or gone crazy! If I keep practicing it will get easier and I will develop more confidence. I am a very worthwhile and valuable person.

One of the tricks with ABCD cards is repetition. The more you write, the easier it becomes. Try and create a card every time you start to feel anxious and your mind begins to race. The other trick is to take your "C"—Consequence—as far out as you possibly can. Make it absurd, make it ridiculous, draw it out to the point where you can laugh at it.

Always Improving

Once a trusted counselor of mine told me that I was the only self-actualized agoraphobic she had ever known. Ever since I was a young adult and realized what that word meant, becoming self-actualized had always been one of my primary goals. However, since I developed this intense anxiety condition which inflicted many limitations on me, I assumed that goal was unreachable. When my counselor made that statement it brought tears to my eyes. I asked her how she thought this was possible, given all the things that were so difficult— if not impossible—for me to do. She replied that being self-actualized simply meant that one was always striving to fulfill their full potential, and it was her belief that was what I was continually trying to do. I am suggesting that we can *all* do that, no matter what our limitations.

In previous chapters, you have heard me talk a lot about simply accepting yourself as you are on any given day. Please understand that this concept in no way conflicts with the concept of improving. It simply means to accept where you are at any given moment and relax with it so you can live your day to its fullest potential and keep moving forward!

Many of us ask "Why am I like this?" While it is not absolutely necessary to discover the answer to that question in order to live a full and rewarding life, you may want to consider any of the following:

1. You may have grown up in an abusive or neglectful environment and learned to become fearful of the world. I know that is at least in part true for me.

2. There may be a genetic predisposition or family history of anxiety disorder.

3. It can be a combination of predisposition and environmental factors, also known as nature versus nurture.

4. The amygdala portion of the brain may be malfunctioning or be of an unusual size and may contribute to extreme fear reactions.

5. You may have experienced a specific traumatic event, such as a serious health crisis, rape or accident, resulting in Post-

Traumatic Stress Disorder (PTSD) which manifests itself as agoraphobia.

As you can see, this is not an exact science. What *is* important is to attempt to discover the coping mechanisms which will enable you to live as full and rewarding a life as possible. Whether your anxiety is a short-term visitor or seems to have moved in permanently, this philosophy holds true in either case.

Looking back, I can clearly see where I have made remarkable strides toward improving my quality of life. I maintain this process to this day—for it is truly a process—and expect I will persist in my endeavors for the rest of my life as I continue to strive for further personal growth and inner peace. While the challenges have been great, the rewards have been just as great. Examples of how I am presently continuing to improve my life include the following scenarios:

1. While I do have a great deal of trouble with social phobia as well as agoraphobia and panic attacks, I continue to try to expand my world and bring people in despite the intense level of discomfort it brings me. I made a conscious choice to work on this particular challenge at this point in my life rather than expand my geographical territory. As there are only so many

things a person can work on at any given time, connecting with others and developing a support system has taken precedence over putting the key in the car. I have discovered ways to get what I need and want from the outside world, but have been sorely lacking in the up close and personal contact with other human beings. Examples of my efforts to stretch in this area are:

A. A friend of mine recently moved here and I allowed her to stay with me for an open-ended amount of time until she found a place to live. That was tough for me since I am severely socially phobic, but I tried to get beyond it in order to extend myself to another. Upon completion of my book, *Behind These Eyes: One Agoraphobic's Journey to a Meaningful Life*, I really came to know that when all is said and done, it is the connections with other people that mean the most.

B. In May of 2014 I initiated the process of bringing in medical specialists to begin to address some health issues I was facing. This was very threatening to me on multiple levels, but I stretched myself and did it anyway. During this time, I had over 30 visits from various health care professionals. I was *way* out of my comfort zone due to the fact that medical problems are on the top of my fear list these days. So, having to have strangers come into my house to deal with medical issues was a double challenge!

C. I keep trying to make new friends and am finally getting more successful in this area. I have recently brought two new people into my life that look like they will become part of a wonderful support system for me. Granted, I have to see them in small increments, but they are willing to work with me and inch by inch my world is beginning to expand once again.

D. I am currently helping the owner of the house behind me get her home ready for remodeling. Since she does not live in the area, I am meeting all kinds of construction people on her behalf. This is an ideal situation for me to practice being around new people because I can come and go freely and only have to see each one for a short period of time.

E. I keep up with old friends who live close enough to visit me. I make sure to invite them to my home for dinner at least occasionally.

F. I keep up with repairs and improvements on my house which requires having new people here from time to time. This is especially difficult for me but I persist in my efforts to improve the quality of my environment.

G. I recently had a reporter from our local newspaper visit to interview me about my book. Although they were not all in person, all together I had about eight interviews. The next step will be having the photographer come to my home. This is a HUGE stretch out of my comfort zone.

1. Developing my spirituality:

I am purposely attempting to develop my spirituality in terms of connecting more fully to this earth to enable me to function better on a day-to-day basis in order to facilitate reaching whatever goals I might have. I do this primarily through reading, taking related college courses online, doing regular meditation and listening to audio books. Again, for me, my inner world is every bit as important—if not more important—than my outer world. Who I am as a human being, how I treat others and what I am able to give of myself is so much more vital than any place I can go outside my home.

2. Progress territorially:

I have it in the back of my mind to try to venture out into the outside world again when I have developed my new support system more fully to the extent that I feel safe and confident with these people.

In conclusion: As with most things, the proof is in the doing. I have achieved many wonderful things in my life despite dealing with the challenges agoraphobia has thrown at me. My accomplishments to date include:

1. Getting my college degree(s).

2. Had a career for over 13 years as a mental health counselor.

3. Owned and operated a T-shirt shop.

4. Presently have a small online business doing custom printing.

5. Acted as caregiver for my mother in my home during the last years of her life.

6. Had some very meaningful love relationships in the past and have currently put my toe back in the water by dating once again.

7. Wrote my memoir and now this handbook.

8. Acted as consultant on two plays and one movie.

9. Currently am having an article written about my life for a large local newspaper.

10. Managed to maintain good health.

11. Have had several lasting friendships.

12. Acted as caregiver for a very close friend until her death.

13. I own a home, car and a rental property.

14. I ran two different support websites at one time.

15. I have wonderful pets.

16. I have managed to run my own life and remain independent.

I believe that my many challenges over the years have made me the person I am today. I believe I was born with a loving heart that still exists within me. I have abandoned my fruitless attempts to swim upstream and have simply made peace with where I am on any given day. I know you can too, no matter where you find yourself.

I once had a psychologist/ medium tell me that she believed the fact that I am still homebound after so many attempts to lead a "normal" life might mean that there is a reason for me to be in this position. Who knows? Maybe I am meant to experience this anxiety disorder to the fullest so I might reach a greater understanding and thereby facilitate healing in others. No matter what the reason, as long as I continue to *accept* where I am I know I will be okay. You will be too if you live each day as it comes and simply do the best you can!

Living with anxiety is like always having a shadow. The trick is to keep your shadow behind you (where it belongs!) Allow it to run in the background and learn to coexist with it. Believe it or not, there is room for both you and your shadow as you live your daily life!

One final thought: Setbacks are a part of *any* recovery. Expect them and do not allow them to deter you on your journey. Do not let them stop you from loving yourself. They are merely bumps in the long road that is your life. Appreciate the setbacks for what they are: proof that you are moving forward. And by all means, keep moving forward!

The trick to love
Now can't you see
Let you be you
Let me be me!

Vive La Difference!

SUGGESTED READING

Arntz, William, Chasse, Betsey and Vincente, Mark. **What the Bleep Do We Know: Discovering the Endless Possibilities for Altering Your Everyday Reality.** Paperback, 2007.

Bourne, Edmund J. **The Anxiety & Phobia Workbook.** New Harbinger Publications, Inc., 1995.

Brach, Tara. **True Refuge: Finding Peace and Freedom in Your Own Awakened Heart** . Bantam, 2013

Buscaglia, Leo F. **Living Loving and Learning.** Ballantine Books, 1985.

Chodron, Pema. **Noble Heart: a Self-guided Retreat on Befriending Your Obstacles.** Sounds True, Inc., 1998.

Chodron, Pema. ***When Things Fall Apart: Heart Advice for Difficult Times.*** Shambhala, 1997.

Chopra, Deepak. ***The Path to Love: Renewing the Power of Spirit in Your Life.*** Harmony, 1996.

Dass, Ram. ***Experiments in Truth.*** Sounds True, Inc., 1998.

Dyer, Wayne. ***Pulling Your Own Strings: Dynamic Techniques for Dealing with Other People and Living Your Life as You Choose.*** William Morrow, 1991.

Gibran, Kahlil. ***The Prophet.*** Alfred A. Knopf, Inc., 1963.

Katie, Byron. ***A Thousand Names for Joy: Living in Harmony with the Way Things Are.*** Crown Archetype, 2007.

MacLaine, Shirley. ***Out on a Limb.*** Bantam, 1986.

McWilliams, Peter. ***You Can't Afford the Luxury of a Negative Thought (The Life 101 Series).*** Mary Book, 1995.

Myss, Caroline. ***Sacred Contracts: Awakening Your Divine Potential.*** Three Rivers Press, 2003.

Rodegast, Pat and Stanton, Judith. ***Emmanuel's Book: A Manuel for Living Comfortably in the Cosmos.*** Bantam, 1987.

Schucman, Helen. *A Course in Miracles.* Foundation for Inner Peace, 1996.

Weekes, Claire, Ph.D. *Peace from Nervous Suffering.* Hawthorn Books, Inc., 1972.

Weil, Andrew. *Breathing: The Master Key to Self-Healing.* Sounds True, Inc., 1991.

Williamson, Marianne. *A Return To Love: Reflections on the Principles of "A Course in Miracles."* Harper Paperbacks, 1996.

Yogananda, Paramahansa. *Autobiography of a Yogi.* Self-Realization Fellowship, 1946.

Made in the USA
Lexington, KY
22 April 2015